Flag Day

Robert
Walker

Crabtree Publishing Company
www.crabtreebooks.com

Crabtree Publishing Company
www.crabtreebooks.com

Author: Robert Walker

Editorial director: Kathy Middleton

Editor: Crystal Sikkens

Photo research: Margaret Amy Salter, Crystal Sikkens

Design: Ken Wright

Cover design: Margaret Amy Salter

Print coordinator: Katherine Berti

Production coordinator: Ken Wright

Prepress technician: Ken Wright

Photographs:
iStockphoto: cover
Library of Congress: pages 18, 19, 21
Shutterstock: pages 4, 7 (left), 8, 27 (bottom); Jason Tench: page 6; Alexandru Cristian Ciobanu: page 7 (right); Matt McClain: page 10; Frances L Fruit: page 30
Thinkstock: pages 1, 5, 23, 25, 26, 27 (top), 29, 31
Wikimedia Commons: page 24; U.S. National Archives and Records Administration: page 9; Cg-realms/ National Atlas of the United States: page 11; Nathaniel Currier: page 12; Philip Dawe: page 13; Makaristos: pages 14, 15; The New Student's Reference Work: page 16; jacobolus: page 17; ourdocuments.gov: page 20 (right); John D. Morris & Co.: page 20 (left); Kurz & Allison: page 22; Youth's Companion/Yale University: page 28

Library and Archives Canada Cataloguing in Publication

Walker, Robert, 1980-
    Flag Day / Robert Walker.

(Celebrations in my world)
Includes index.
Issued also in electronic format.
ISBN 978-0-7787-4087-2 (bound).--ISBN 978-0-7787-4092-6 (pbk.)

    1. Flag Day--Juvenile literature. 2. United States--History--Revolution, 1775-1783--Juvenile literature. 3. Flags--United States--History--Juvenile literature. 4. Flags--Juvenile literature. I. Title. II. Series: Celebrations in my world

JK1761.W35 2012   j394.263   C2012-900902-4

Library of Congress Cataloging-in-Publication Data

Walker, Robert, 1980-
Flag day / Robert Walker.
p. cm. -- (Celebrations in my world)
Includes index.
ISBN 978-0-7787-4087-2 (reinforced library binding : alk. paper) --
ISBN 978-0-7787-4092-6 (pbk. : alk. paper) -- ISBN 978-1-4271-7846-6
(electronic pdf) -- ISBN 978-1-4271-7961-6 (electronic html)
1. Flag Day--Juvenile literature. I. Title.

JK1761.W35 2012
394.262--dc23
                        2012004071

Crabtree Publishing Company
www.crabtreebooks.com   1-800-387-7650

Printed in the U.S.A./052012/FA20120413

Published in Canada
Crabtree Publishing
616 Welland Ave.
St. Catharines, Ontario
L2M 5V6

Published in the United States
Crabtree Publishing
PMB 59051
350 Fifth Avenue, 59th Floor
New York, New York 10118

Published in the United Kingdom
Crabtree Publishing
Maritime House
Basin Road North, Hove
BN41 1WR

Published in Australia
Crabtree Publishing
3 Charles Street
Coburg North
VIC 3058

Contents

A Very Special Day

Flag Day is the **anniversary** of the creation of the flag for the United States of America. This important day is celebrated across the country every year on June 14. The U.S. flag was first made over 200 years ago in 1777.

Some European flags are almost 1000 years old. This makes the 200-year-old U.S. flag seem young!

DID YOU KNOW?

Another name for the United States' flag is Old Glory. It is believed the name was given to the flag by ship Captain Stephen Driver in 1831.

The 13 colonies were the first areas of land settled by British colonists in North America.

The United States' flag is known as the Stars and Stripes. This is because of the rows of red and white stripes on the flag and the collection of stars in the top left corner. The 13 stripes represent the first colonies in the United States, and the 50 stars are for the 50 U.S. states.

What is a Flag?

Flags are all around us. They have different names, such as banner, pennant, standard, and ensign. They are found in different colors with different shapes and **symbols**. All countries have their own flag, as well as states, cities, armies and different groups.

Sports teams have flags with the team's logo on it. These flags are waved during a game to show support for the team.

DID YOU KNOW?

Flags have been used for thousands of years. The earliest ones were made of wood.

• Flags can be hung from a pole or carried by people at special events.

Flags are usually made of cloth. The symbols and colors on them have an important meaning to the place or group the flag represents. For example, the state of Wyoming features a bison. This animal was very important to the survival of the early people of the area.

The First Flag Day

The first day to honor the Stars and Stripes was in 1877. This marked the 100th anniversary of the flag's birthday. The United States Congress, the part of government that makes the laws for the country, ordered all public buildings to fly the flag to celebrate the occasion.

- Most public buildings, including libraries, government buildings, town halls, and recreation areas, not only fly the flag on Flag Day, but year round.

In 1885, a school teacher named Bernard J. Cigrand decided there should be an official day to celebrate the flag every year. He began writing letters to newspapers, magazines, and members of government. Groups such as the **National Flag Day Association** were created, asking the government to declare an official flag day.

- In 1949, U.S. President Harry S. Truman signed a law officially making June 14 Flag Day.

DID YOU KNOW?

To pay tribute to someone who has died, a flag will be raised only halfway up a flagpole. This is called flying the flag at half-staff or half-mast.

9

The Thirteen Colonies

After Christopher Columbus landed in 1492, Europeans began coming to North America in search of new land. In 1607, Great Britain started to establish large settlements called colonies to increase its control of North America.

The colonies became part of the **British Empire** and had t[o] follow British rules and laws.

DID YOU KNOW?

North and South America were called the "New World" by Europeans. These were new land discoveries made by European explorers.

Great Britain founded 13 colonies along the east coast of North America.

They were Massachusetts, Maryland, Connecticut, North Carolina, South Carolina, New Jersey, New Hampshire, Pennsylvania, Georgia, Rhode Island, Virginia, New York, and Delaware.

- Virginia was the first colony, founded in 1607, and Georgia was the last founded, in 1733.

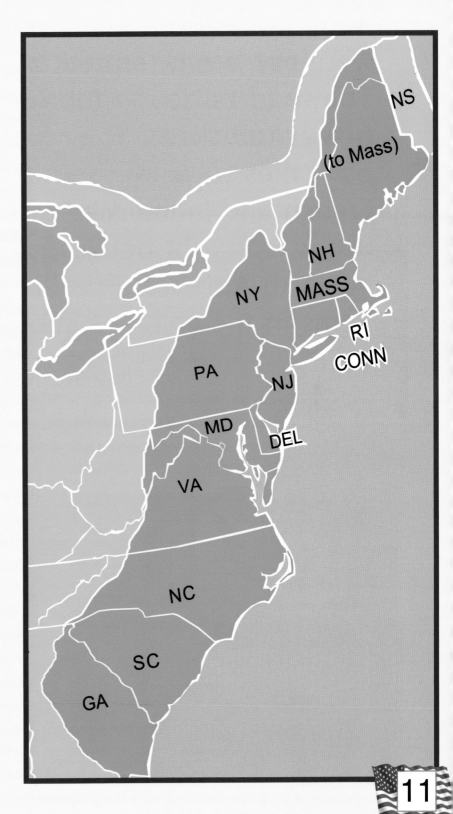

Troubles With Britain

As time went on, many colonists felt they were not being treated fairly by Britain. They had no say in the rules and laws that **governed** them. They were also forced to pay taxes to Britain to help pay for the French and Indian War of 1754–1763. The war was fought between Britain and France in North America. Britain taxed popular items in the colonies such as tea and paper.

Upset by the tax on tea, a group of colonists, some dressed as Native Americans, stormed the Boston harbor and dumped boatloads of tea into the water. This became known as the Boston Tea Party.

Britain responded to the Boston Tea Party **protest** by creating the five Coercive Acts. The colonists named these the "Intolerable Acts." The Acts were laws that punished the colonists for taking action against British laws. Outraged, the leaders of the Thirteen Colonies decided, in 1775, that it was time to cut ties with Britain.

- This illustration shows colonists "**tarring and feathering**" a representative of the king as a protest.

DID YOU KNOW?

The Sugar Act of 1764 taxed anything made from sugar. This led to molasses smuggling among the colonies.

Flags of the American Revolution

Going into battle with Britain, the American troops, known as the **Continental Army**, needed a flag. One of the first American independence flags was the Grand Union flag. It had the same 13 red and white stripes as the U.S. flag does today. It also had a small British flag in the corner.

The Grand Union flag was first flown on ships in December 1775 and on land on January 1, 1776.

There were many other colonist flags that were flown during the American Revolution. Some represented where the colonists were from, others showed the names of the different **battalions**, or groups of soldiers. There were also different flags used by colonists who fought on land and those who fought on the water.

- The Bennington flag has a 76 on it representing the year 1776, when the **Declaration of Independence** was signed.

DID YOU KNOW?

The British flag is called the Union Jack. A "jack" is a tiny version of a flag that is flown on the front of a ship to show its country of origin.

15

The Flag Act

It was soon decided by the Continental Congress, the first American government, that there needed to be one official flag for all of the colonies to use. In 1777, the new American government passed the very first Flag Act.

- The official flag was flown for the first time at Fort Staniwix, now Rome, N.Y., on August 2, 1777.

DID YOU KNOW?

Philadelphia, Pennsylvania, was where the first American government was located.

The Flag Act declared that America's official flag would have 13 red and white stripes, with 13 stars in a blue square in the upper left corner. This would make the design of the nation's flag look the same way across the country. As the number of states increased, more Flag Acts were created to add the extra stars to the flag.

- The arrangement of the stars was not specified in the first Flag Act, so different designs were used in different places.

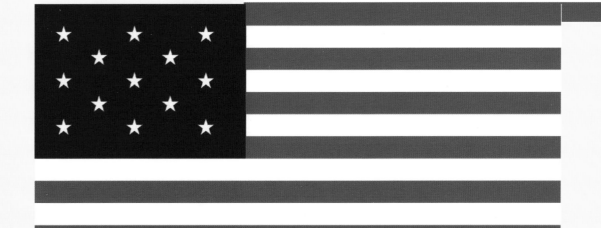

Betsy Ross Gets Sewing

Betsy Ross was a very talented **seamstress**. In 1773, Betsy and her husband John started a business in Philadelphia. They made and sold fabrics for clothes, furniture, flags, and curtains.

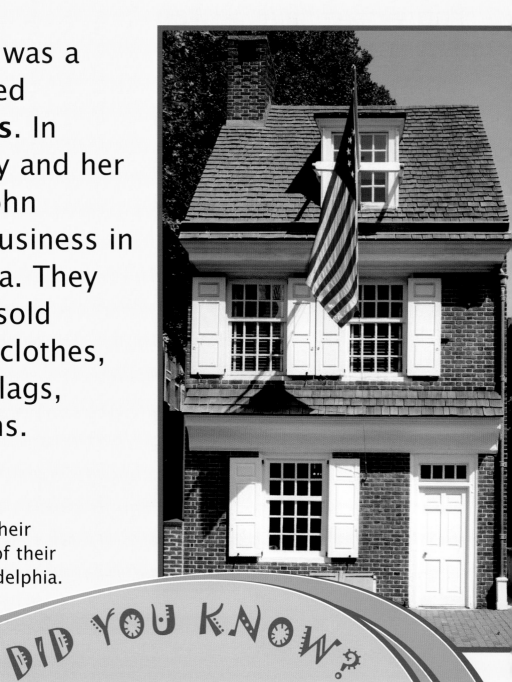

● Betsy and her husband ran their business out of their home in Philadelphia.

DID YOU KNOW?

Betsy Ross' real name was Elizabeth. Betsy was a nickname Elizabeth's parents had given her as a little girl.

Betsy and her family attended the same church as George Washington, who became the leader of the Continental Army when the American Revolution began. It is believed that George Washington asked Betsy Ross to make the flag for the revolting colonists.

- The state stars in the Betsy Ross flag were placed in a circle. This was meant to show that no state was more important than the rest.

The Birth of a Nation

The American Revolution came to an end in 1783. Many colonists as well as British soldiers lost their lives in the fighting. Even though the colonists had less soldiers and weapons, they managed to defeat the British troops.

- The American Revolution was brought to an end with the signing of the Treaty of Paris. It declared the United States to be an independent nation.

Many people think the colonists were able to defeat the British because they felt so strongly about their cause. They were fighting for the right to govern their own country. The Stars and Stripes flag reminded the colonists of what they were fighting for.

- George Washington led the Continental Army to victory against the British.

DID YOU KNOW?

During the American Revolution, colonists who wanted to stay under British control were called "loyalists." The colonists who rebelled were called "patriots."

The Right Way to Use the Flag

The Flag Code is a set of rules telling people how to handle and display the American flag. One of the most important rules is that the flag should never touch the ground. This tradition began on the battlefield. A soldier known as the color bearer was in charge of carrying the flag. If he was killed, another soldier was expected to pick up the flag and continue the charge.

The U.S. flag was a sign of encouragement to soldiers on the field. It was also used to control troop movement.

When the American flag is hanging, it has to be higher than any other flags nearby. The only exception is at the **United Nations**, where the flags of countries from around the world are treated equally. The U.S. flag should not be displayed upside down or have anything attached to it, such as buttons or streamers.

At military funerals, a flag is placed on top of the casket. It has to be removed and properly folded before the burial.

DID YOU KNOW?

Regular ships will dip their country's flag when passing a naval ship. The naval ship will respond the same way as a greeting.

Our Flag Today

America's flag has gone though many changes. Most changes were to increase the number of stars as more states joined the **Union**. The Flag Act of 1794, however, increased the number of red and white stripes to 15. The number was changed back to 13 in 1818.

- The 15-stripe flag was used during the War of 1812 when the Americans were at war with the British.

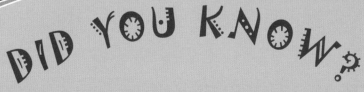

*The white of the flag stands for purity. The red for **valor**, or bravery. The blue stands for justice.*

The last change to the flag happened in 1960 when the 50th state, Hawaii, joined the Union. Today's flag now has the stars arranged in nine offset rows and eleven offset columns. The flag can be made at any size, but the stars and stripes have to be the right **proportions** and the length of the flag has to be 0.9 percent larger than the height.

People can buy the American flag in all different sizes. The flags made for government use, however, are made at a standard size.

25

Celebrating Flag Day

Americans recognize the importance of their flag on June 14 every year. Across the country there are parades, speeches, and other gatherings to mark the occasion. The U.S. Army's birthday is also celebrated on this day. The army was founded on June 14, 1775.

- Flag-raising ceremonies are a very important part of Flag Day.

DID YOU KNOW?

During the War of 1812, Mary Pickersgill made a huge flag for forces at Fort McHenry—nearly 30 by 42 feet (9 by 13 meters) in size!

Since 1966 there has been a National Flag Week in the United States, running from June 14 to June 20. People are encouraged to fly a flag at home for the whole week. Other colorful decorations such as bunting are very popular.

- Bunting is a decoration often hung on houses that displays the U.S. flag's colors, stars, and stripes.

The Pledge of Allegiance

The best way to honor Flag Day is with the Pledge of Allegiance. The Pledge of Allegiance was written in 1892 by Francis Bellamy. He wrote it to celebrate the 400th anniversary of Columbus landing in America. The pledge honors the flag as well as the people and the nation's beliefs behind it. Bellamy sent the pledge to schools across the country for students to learn.

- Francis Bellamy published the Pledge of Allegiance in *The Youth's Companion*, a very popular magazine for children at the time.

In 1954, the words "under God" were added to the pledge. Since then the pledge has not been changed. It is written as follows:

"I pledge allegiance to the flag of the United States of America, and to the Republic for which it stands, one nation under God, indivisible, with liberty and justice for all."

- The Pledge of Allegiance is said while facing the flag with your right hand over your heart.

DID YOU KNOW?

Some schools in the United States have students say the Pledge of Allegiance every day.

Get Involved!

There are plenty of ways for you to take part in Flag Day. You can ask your parents to go to a parade or flag-raising ceremony in your area. Many community groups such as veterans' organizations also hold events on Flag Day that the public is welcome to attend.

You might even be able to take part in one of the events in your community.

DID YOU KNOW?

Since 1996, Canada has celebrated its own National Flag Day on February 15.

You can also celebrate Flag Day by making your own flag. Ask your friends to help you create your own Stars and Stripes using markers, colored pencils, or cutting out colored paper. You could also make some other colorful Flag Day decorations. Just be sure to include the important colors from the flag—red, white, and blue.

Once you're done making your own flag, ask your friends to help you name each state that the 50 stars represent.

Glossary

anniversary The celebration of an event on the day it took place in the years following it

battalion A group of soldiers that are prepared to fight

British Empire A large empire that included Great Britain and the territories under its control

Continental Army The first colonist soldiers that got together to fight the British

govern To watch over and control a group of people

National Flag Day Association A group that carries on the patriotic work of Bernard J. Cigrand

proportion The size, number, or amount of something in relation to another

protest An action taken to show disagreement or displeasure

seamstress A woman who sews

symbol Something that represents something else

tarring and feathering Painting tar on a person and sticking feathers to the tar as a punishment

Union The collection of states

United Nations An international group of countries that promotes peace and cooperation

Index